~~Faster than a speeding bullet~~

~~More powerful than a locomotive~~

~~Look! Up in the sky!~~

Bird....

DC Comics

Karen Berger *VP – Executive Editor*
Pornsak Pichetshote *Assistant Editor*
Amie Brockway-Metcalf *Art Director*
Paul Levitz *President & Publisher*
Georg Brewer *VP - Design & Retail Product Development*
Richard Bruning *Sr. VP - Creative Director*
Patrick Caldon *Sr. VP - Finance & Operations*
Chris Caramalis *VP-Finance*
Terri Cunningham *VP-Managing Editor*
Dan DiDio *VP-Editorial*
Alison Gill *VP – Manufacturing*
Lillian Laserson *Sr. VP & General Counsel*
Jim Lee *Editorial Director - WildStorm*
David McKillips *VP – Advertising & Custom Publishing*
John Nee *VP – Business Development*
Gregory Noveck *Sr. VP – Creative Affairs*
Cheryl Rubin *VP- Brand Management*
Bob Wayne *VP – Sales & Marketing*

It's a Bird...

hc isbn 1-4012-0109-1
sc isbn 1-4012-0311-6

cover artist Teddy Kristiansen
logo design Pete Friedrich

Day of Admittance

May 5.

Diagnosis

...GTON'S

...MARKS/TESTS...

WHAT I THINK ABOUT **MOST**
IS THE BIG RED **S**...

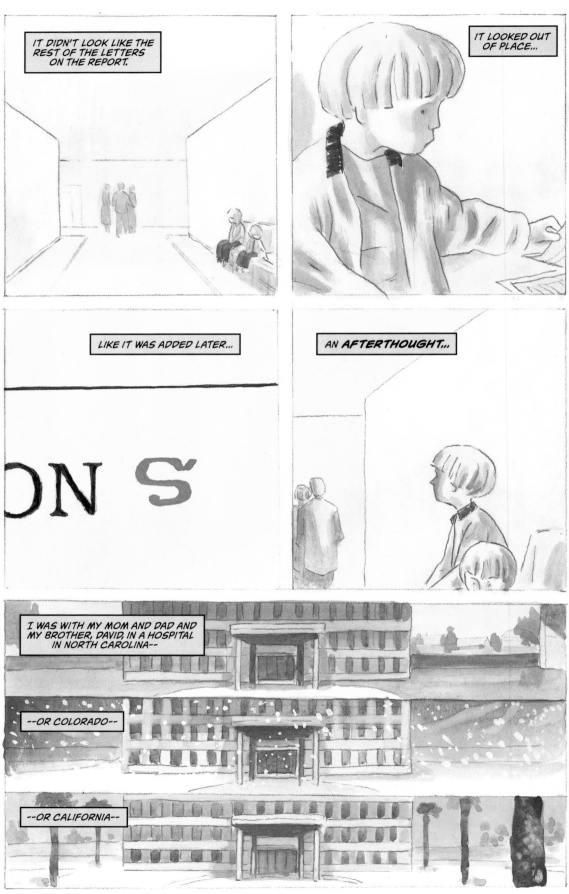

IT DIDN'T LOOK LIKE THE REST OF THE LETTERS ON THE REPORT.

IT LOOKED OUT OF PLACE...

LIKE IT WAS ADDED LATER...

AN *AFTERTHOUGHT*...

ON S

I WAS WITH MY MOM AND DAD AND MY BROTHER, DAVID, IN A HOSPITAL IN NORTH CAROLINA--

--OR COLORADO--

--OR CALIFORNIA--

4

THE COSTUME

SEVENTH GRADE WAS WHERE IT ALL STARTED TO GET WEIRD. SOME OF THE BOYS LOOKED LIKE KIDS, WHILE THEIR FRIENDS THE SAME AGE LOOKED LIKE MEN.

SOME OF THE GIRLS STILL PLAYED WITH DOLLS, BUT OTHERS BEGAN TO DRESS LIKE THEIR OLDER SISTERS.

AND THINGS THAT DIDN'T USED TO MATTER SUDDENLY DID.

THE KIDS CONGREGATED INTO GROUPS THAT WOULD ENDURE UNTIL GRADUATION DAY: THE JOCKS...THE BRAINS...THE GEEKS.

UNFORTUNATELY, JASON DOBSON WASN'T LUCKY ENOUGH TO FIT IN WITH ANY OF THEM. HE SAT ALONE AT LUNCH, PAINFULLY AWARE THAT EVEN THE GEEKS HAD SOMEONE TO EAT WITH.

JASON DOBSON SAT IN THE BACK OF CLASS ANSWERING HISTORY QUESTIONS WRONG.

JASON DOBSON STOOD UP TO GET ANOTHER "D" ON ANOTHER MATH QUIZ. JASON DOBSON WAITED IN SHOP CLASS FOR MR. SPIRO TO REMEMBER HIS NAME. IT ALWAYS TOOK A MINUTE LONGER THAN IT SHOULD HAVE.

BUT EVERYTHING WAS DIFFERENT THE DAY THAT JASON DOBSON CHANGED HIS IDENTITY... OCTOBER 31ST... HALLOWEEN. HE DIDN'T GET A NEW HAIRCUT...

...HE GOT A NEW SUIT. AND FOR ONE GRAND MORNING, THE GIRLS THOUGHT HE WAS CUTE AND THE GUYS JOKED WITH HIM LIKE BUDDIES.

JASON DOBSON WAS A STAR.

HIS SPIRIT FLEW. FOR THAT ONE LONG AFTERNOON, HE WAS SOME- ONE. JASON DOBSON WAS SUPERMAN.

BUT THE NEXT DAY, BACK IN HIS HAND-ME-DOWN CLOTHES AND INDUSTRIAL-STRENGTH GLASSES, HE WASN'T A HERO...OR A JOCK...OR A BRAIN... OR EVEN A GEEK. HE WAS SOMETHING FAR WORSE.

HE WAS JASON DOBSON AGAIN.

SO ONE WEEK LATER, HE MADE A BOLD--IF NOT DESPERATE--DECISION. HE WORE THE COSTUME TO SCHOOL ONCE MORE. BUT IT WASN'T HALLOWEEN. IT WAS THURSDAY. AND NOW JASON WASN'T CUTE, HE WAS WEIRD.

WEIRDER THAN 7TH GRADE.

AND THIS TIME WHEN MR. SPIRO TOOK TOO LONG TO REMEMBER HIS NAME, IT WASN'T TO GIVE HIM A FAILING GRADE ON HIS SPICE RACK PROJECT. IT WAS TO SEND HIM TO THE PRINCIPAL'S OFFICE TO EXPLAIN WHY HE WAS "DRESSED LIKE A CARTOON."

ON THE WAY, HE MET UP WITH SOME LEX LUTHORS-- KIDS WHO PLANNED ON RULING SOCIETY *NOW* SINCE THEY WOULD HAVE LITTLE POWER ONCE THEY LEFT PUBLIC SCHOOL. JASON DOBSON COULDN'T SAVE THE EARTH. HE COULDN'T EVEN SAVE HIMSELF.

A SUIT LIKE THAT DIDN'T FIT IN WITH A WORLD LIKE THIS. BUT WHY? WASN'T EVERYONE'S CLOTHING A COSTUME OF ONE KIND OR ANOTHER? THE JOCKS, THE BRAINS, THE GEEKS?

JASON DOBSON CLIMBED TO THE TOP OF THE SCHOOL'S MAIN STAIRWELL.

MAYBE HE THOUGHT HE COULD GET AWAY. MAYBE HE THOUGHT HE COULD FLY. MAYBE HE THOUGHT A QUICK EXIT WOULD AT LEAST MAKE HIM SOMEONE FOR ONE LAST AFTERNOON.

BUT BEFORE HE COULD TEST ANY OF NEWTON'S LAWS OR SUPERMAN'S SKILLS--THE BIOLOGY TEACHER, MRS. KAUFMAN, PROVED TO JASON DOBSON THAT SCIENCE...

...IS MORE TANGIBLE THAN FANTASY.

JASON DOBSON CAME BACK TO SCHOOL AFTER TWO WEEKS OF SUSPENSION, WELL AWARE THAT HE WOULD NEVER BE "SUPER" AGAIN.

WHAT IS IT?

NOTHING.

THIS IS THE LOOK LISA GIVES ME WHEN I'M NOT TELLING HER ENOUGH.

I GET THIS LOOK A *LOT*.

I KNOW SHE RESENTS THAT I'M KEEPING THIS TO MYSELF, BUT I'VE GOT TO BE *HONEST*. WHEN I WAS A KID, MY PARENTS WERE AFRAID--

--OR MAYBE THE RIGHT WORD IS *"ASHAMED"*...TO TALK ABOUT "THE FAMILY SECRET."

A SECRET WHISPERED THAT DAY AT THE *HOSPITAL*...

...THE DAY I WAS BEING BABY-SAT BY HALF A *SUPERMAN* COMIC...

...THERE WAS TENSION BREWING JUST BEYOND THE PANEL BORDERS.

AT THE TIME, MY DAD WAS IN THE AIR FORCE.

WE LIVED OUT OF STATE AND NO ONE HAD EVEN CALLED TO TELL US GRANDMA WAS SICK.

I COULDN'T HEAR *EVERYTHING* THEY WERE SAYING, BUT I STRAINED AND CAUGHT A LITTLE BIT THAT STOOD OUT--

...WHEN DID YOU *KNOW?*

THE OUTSIDER

Suit and Tie
Hat and Glasses
Clark Kent fits
    right in
To the Walk-a-day
Work-a-day
Chit-chat
Clickity-clack
Paycheck and
    Collar-stay
Water-cooler
    world of
    Metropolis.

On that Oh-so-
    anticipated
    Lunch Break
There's always
    time for a
    Quick Change
A Quick Flight
Quick Work
For Would-be
    World-crushers
And then right
    back to
Suit and Tie
Hat and Glasses
Oh yes, Clark Kent
    fits right in.

But down in
    Accounting
Columns and Rows
And Linda Goldberg
    knows
The "Ha ha ha's" at
    the Water Cooler
Are Jokes about
    how "Her People"
Are always "the ones
    handling Money."
No Lunch Break
    long enough
To allow her a
    Quick Change
From her Heritage
    or its Critics.

Leather gloves
Denim fatigues
If DeRon Sanford
   didn't come to
   work
Everyone on The
   Planet would
   Notice
But when he Does
   come in
He doesn't Blend in
So much as
   Vanish in
Push and Sweep
   Plain Sight
The Invisible Man.

Until the Coffee
   Club Money
Goes Missing from
   Someone's Desk
No one looks at Clark,
   or even Linda
They don't say a Word
But don't really
   have to
And on his
   Lunch Break
There's no way
   DeRon can
Push and Sweep
   away the Skin
That makes him live
   Outside Himself.

And Greg Giddley
Whose legs are
   Aluminum Spokes
And Melissa
   Bandeau
Whose "Boyfriend"
   isn't a Boy at all
Join the Staff that
   Searches each
   day
For Suit and Tie
Hat and Glasses
That will bring
   them from the
   Outside
In.

WELL IT *IS*...

...A NASTY LITTLE DISEASE THAT EATS AWAY AT THE NERVOUS SYSTEM UNTIL THERE'S NO CONTROLLING IT.

FOR A FEW YEARS, I WROTE SOME "MUTANT" COMICS-- TRYING TO THINK OF EXCITING NEW *POWERS* THE HEROES' SECRET GENETIC STRUCTURES MIGHT GIVE THEM.

I QUIT WHEN I REALIZED THAT SOME GENES DON'T *GIVE* POWERS...

...THEY TAKE POWERS *AWAY.*

THE POWER TO *WALK.*

THE POWER TO *SIT UP.*

THE POWER TO *EAT.*

THE POWER TO *SPEAK.*

MY PARENTS NEVER SPOKE MUCH ABOUT WHAT HAD KILLED MY GRAND- MOTHER.

THEY JUST SAID WHAT THEY KNEW:

THAT IT DAMAGES *NERVES* AND RUNS IN *FAMILIES.*

UNFORTUNATELY, WHAT THEY KNEW WASN'T MUCH BECAUSE HUNTINGTON'S CHOREA ISN'T A *GLAMOUR* DISEASE.

OKAY!

NOT ENOUGH *CASUALTIES.* NO *CELEBRITIES* HAVE DIED FROM IT...

...JUST PEOPLE LIKE MY *GRANDMOTHER.*

28

LEAVING KRYPTON (Life on another world)

IN 1938 THE INFANT KAL-EL LEFT HIS HOMEWORLD OF KRYPTON.

OF COURSE HE HAD TO.

HE TRAVELED FOR LIGHT-YEARS--

--AND GOT AS FAR FROM HOME AS A BOY COULD GET--

--KANSAS--

--WHICH, THOUGH LIKE NOTHING ON EARTH--

--CONFIRMED THAT THE YOUNG KRYPTONIAN WOULD FIND THE HELP NEEDED--

--FROM LIFE ON ANOTHER WORLD.

IT'S AN APPEALING NOTION--

--LEAVE WHERE YOU'RE FROM AND START OVER SOMEPLACE ELSE.

IT WAS THE PROMISE OF COLUMBUS--

--AND THE LURE OF APOLLO.

BUT COLUMBUS DIED BEFORE ACTUALLY SETTING FOOT ON AMERICAN SOIL.

AND NOT ALL ASTRONAUTS EMBRACE ETHEREAL SPACE IN THE WAY THEY HOPE TO.

THERE ARE MANY WAYS TO LEAVE THE WORLD BEHIND--

--BUT ONLY ONE THAT EVER HAD A PERFECT ENDING.

30

31

INVULNERABLE

IN ACTION COMICS #1, JERRY SIEGEL AND JOE SHUSTER DECLARED THEIR MAN *"SUPER!"* INVULNERABLE.

BUT DID THEY MEAN THAT HE COULDN'T BE HARMED... OR THAT HE CAN'T BE TOUCHED?

BECAUSE THE FORMER IS EXTREMELY USEFUL FOR A HERO, WHILE THE LATTER IS A FATAL FLAW FOR ANY MAN, SUPER OR OTHERWISE.

BUT HOW COULD SOMETHING "INVULNERABLE" ALSO BE FLAWED?

ACHILLES CAN ANSWER THAT QUESTION.

DIPPED BY HIS MOTHER IN THE RIVER STYX, HE TOO BECAME INVULNERABLE.

BUT WHILE HE WAS A LEADER OF GREAT ARMIES AND THE HERO OF THE TROJAN WARS--

--IT TURNED OUT HE WAS JUST A HEEL, SUSCEPTIBLE WHERE HE HAD BEEN...

...DUNKED.

IN 221 B.C., THERE WAS NO KRYPTON AND ALL A MAN NEEDED TO BE INVULNERABLE WAS A GREAT WALL--

--THIRTY FEET THICK, 1500 MILES LONG AND VISIBLE FROM SPACE.

BUT THE GREAT WALL TURNED OUT TO BE MANY SEPARATE STRUCTURES WITH VAST, INDEFENSIBLE GAPS BETWEEN THEM.

AND CENTURIES LATER, NASA ASTRONAUTS LOOKING DOWN ON IT FROM THE HEAVENS SAW NOTHING BUT CHINA.

THERE WAS ONLY ONE INVINCIBLE ALEXANDER THE GREAT, BUT HE DIED OF A FEVER WHILE PLOTTING IN BABYLON.

THERE WAS ONLY ONE UNSINKABLE TITANIC, BUT IT PROVED NO STRONGER THAN THE ICE FLOES OF THE NORTH ATLANTIC.

THERE IS ONLY ONE CLARK KENT AND EVEN HE HAS HIS ACHILLES HEEL, HIS TITANIC FLAW...

...HIS INVULNERABILITY EFFECTIVE ONLY IN PULP PAPER FICTION.

KRYPTONITE

DANGER!

BEWARE!

KRYPTONITE!

FEELING LIKE THERE'S *NO WAY* TO *DEFEAT* THE *ULTIMATE MAN?!* *YOU'RE RIGHT!*

SO WHY NOT DIG UP A SPECIAL LITTLE *SOMETHING* THAT MAKES IT *SUPER-SIMPLE?!*

KRYPTONITE!

STOPS THE ULTIMATE MAN... *DEAD IN HIS TRACKS!*

KRYPTONITE!

AVAILABLE IN *TWO* ACTION-FRIENDLY *COLORS!*

KRYP-TO-NITE!

HOW DOES IT WORK?

WHAT IF--AND STICK *WITH* US ON THIS ONE!--WHAT IF THE PLANET *KRYPTON* SENT OFF *SHARDS* OF ITSELF WHEN IT *EXPLODED?!*

AND WHAT IF THOSE *SHARDS* WERE LIKE *POISON* TO ANY-ONE WHO USED TO *LIVE* ON KRYPTON AS A *BABY?!*

STUPID!

HON...?

NO, YOU CAN'T HELP!

DON'T BARK AT ME. **SOMETHING'S** MAKING YOU ANGRY-- YOU'RE MAKING **ME** ANGRY!

TELL ME WHAT IT IS. **TALK** TO ME.

MAYBE I CAN HELP IF YOU DON'T SHUT ME OUT.

NOW...YOU HAD AN IDEA AND EVERYTHING WAS GREAT. THEN SOMETHING HAPPENED...?

HE THOUGHT I COULDN'T HEAR WHAT HE SAID, BUT I **DID** HEAR...

...KRYPTONITE...

...EVERY WORD...

I'LL TELL YOU WHAT HAPPENED! **KRYPTONITE** IS ANTI-THETICAL TO SUPERMAN! IT'S THE **OPPOSITE** OF LIFE.

SOME SICK BASTARD WROTE THE WORD "KRYPTONITE," AND SUDDENLY SUPERMAN IS **VULNERABLE!**

AREN'T WE ALL?

COME TO BED. COME AND RUB MY FEET. NO REASON WE SHOULD **BOTH** BE MISERABLE.

EVERYTHING WILL LOOK BETTER IN THE MORNING.

RED, YELLOW, BLUE

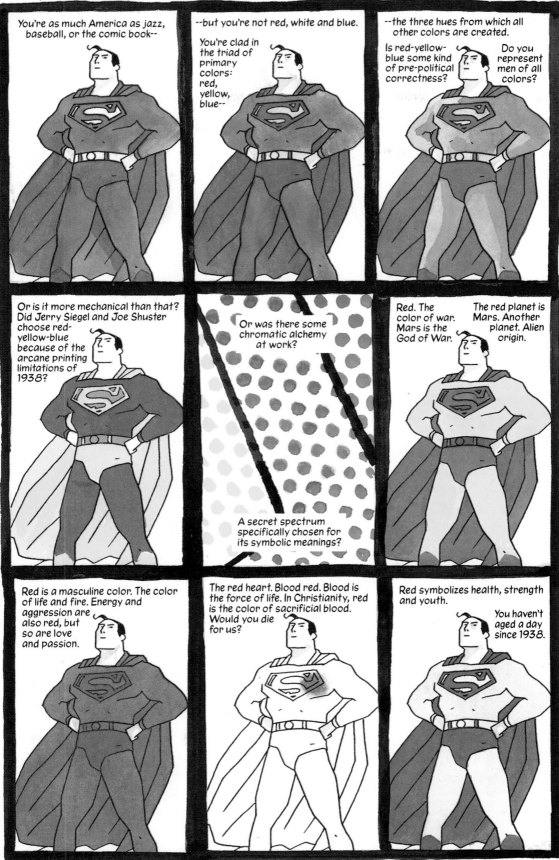

You're as much America as jazz, baseball, or the comic book--

--but you're not red, white and blue.

You're clad in the triad of primary colors: red, yellow, blue--

--the three hues from which all other colors are created.

Is red-yellow-blue some kind of pre-political correctness?

Do you represent men of all colors?

Or is it more mechanical than that? Did Jerry Siegel and Joe Shuster choose red-yellow-blue because of the arcane printing limitations of 1938?

Or was there some chromatic alchemy at work?

A secret spectrum specifically chosen for its symbolic meanings?

Red. The color of war. Mars is the God of War.

The red planet is Mars. Another planet. Alien origin.

Red is a masculine color. The color of life and fire. Energy and aggression are also red, but so are love and passion.

The red heart. Blood red. Blood is the force of life. In Christianity, red is the color of sacrificial blood. Would you die for us?

Red symbolizes health, strength and youth.

You haven't aged a day since 1938.

43

SMALLVILLE

It was that perfect stretch of July. Hurricane eye of the harvest season—the calm center between planting and picking. Summer vacation for a Smallville farmer's son.

But an ocean of hay against a shimmering barley beach made staying at home an unendurable holiday. "Go," his adoptive father told him. "I know you want to head to town for the movies, so go. But Clark? Don't forget who you are."

Don't forget who you are... his father was always saying things like this. Simple stories with complex morals. "Pay the most heed to folks who speak the least." "Work fast, but never so fast you have to work twice."

They were fertile little lessons sewn in sparse parcels of words. Sometimes they seemed too simple to even be meaningful. but later they'd reverberate back on him...

...more than they did at first hearing.

For so many years he'd had to be less than he was, hide his abilities from his classmates and the good people of Smallville. But now his father had said, "Be yourself. Go to town as you really are! Fly if you're able. Don't forget who you are!" It was a grant of independence.

But it was a short-lived liberation as, his head in the clouds, his father's words turned back on him—a gust of realization. "Don't forget who you are," suddenly meant two things: Remember your heritage, yes, but also... don't lose sight of who you have become.

Because once the townsfolk saw him flying, once they knew he was not like them, once he'd crossed that line...

...he could never be just a farmer's son again. True, that day would almost certainly come, but now he realized he should choose its arrival carefully.

And so he walked the rest of the way to town, a part of his surroundings rather than above them. A full hour at a normal human pace, he knew he'd miss the first half of the movie, but he'd leave home a boy, and arrive in Smallville a man.

WHEN I GOT OLDER, IT OCCURRED TO ME WHY AUNT SARAH INTERRUPTED.

THE DISEASE WASN'T SOMETHING ONE *SPOKE* OF.

IT WAS AN *EMBARRASSMENT.* BUT *WHY?*

AIN'T NO ONE HERE BUT THE GHOSTS AND SPIDERS, AMIGO.

WHY'D WE COME IF YOUR AUNT'S BEEN *GONE* SO LONG?

I DIDN'T KNOW SHE'D MOVED. MY DAD DISAPPEARED ONCE BEFORE.... HE'D COME *HERE* TO STAY WITH HER.

WAS SHE A *CRACK-HEAD* OR SOMETHIN'? THIS PLACE IS A *DUMP.*

IT WASN'T LIKE THIS BACK THEN. IT WAS NICER.

Y'KNOW, I STILL DON'T GET WHY DAD CAME HERE. WHEN HE CAME BACK HOME, NOTHING WAS EVER SAID ABOUT IT.

SOMETHING MUST'VE *HAPPENED.*

YEAH. SHE PACKED UP AND MOVED, BUT FORGOT THE "PACKED UP" PART.

ANYWAY, SHE AIN'T HERE AND NEITHER IS YOUR POPS. SO WHAT NEXT?

WANNA MEET THE GUY WHO'S WRITING SUPERMAN *NOW?*

JOE ALLEN?!

I TOLD HIM WE'D GRAB A CONEY DOG WITH HIM IF YOU HAD THE TIME.

TO MEET *JOE ALLEN?!* I'LL *MAKE* TIME!

CLICHÉS LIKE, "YOU CAN'T GO HOME AGAIN"? THEY'RE COMPLETELY BONE-ACHINGLY TRUE.

THAT'S HOW THEY GET TO BE CLICHÉS.

ANOTHER TRUE CLICHE..."IT'S A SMALL WORLD."

IT'S FUNNY, EDITORS THINK WRITERS AND ARTISTS DON'T KNOW EACH OTHER, BUT WE *DO.*

JEREMY'S WORKED WITH JOE *WAY* LONGER THAN ME, BUT HE DOESN'T GET THAT I KNOW JOE *TOO,* SO I KNOW ALL ABOUT JEREMY'S LITTLE QUIRKS AS A BOSS.

IF AN EDITOR SAYS SOMETHING TO A FREELANCER, THE REST OF US KNOW ABOUT IT AN HOUR LATER. THERE ARE NO SECRETS IN OUR INDUSTRY.

COMICS ARE BETTER THAN LIFE IN *THAT* REGARD.

STEVE! HOWZIT GOIN', MAN?

JOE? RAFA. RAFA? THIS IS JOE ALLEN. DEPARTING WRITER OF--

SUPERMAN VERSUS THE JLA. WHO WINS?

EASY. SUPES.

PLEASURE TO MEET YOU.

SO THEY OFFERED YOU THE BOOK, HUH? COULDN'T FALL IN BETTER HANDS. EXCITED?

NOT REALLY. I DON'T GET THE APPEAL OF SUPERMAN. NEVER HAVE.

NO WAY! YOU'RE A SMART GUY. YOU DON'T SEE THE GRAND DESIGN?

ENLIGHTEN ME.

WELL....I KNOW HOW YOU THINK. YOU'RE PROBABLY HUNG UP ON SUPES'S LACK OF INTELLECTUAL *SOUNDNESS*-- BUT IT'S ACTUALLY PRETTY *TIGHT.*

AT THE TIME OF SUPES'S *CREATION*, YOU HAD IMMIGRANTS LEAVING *EUROPE* IN HOPES OF A BETTER LIFE IN *AMERICA* AND--

--YOU HAD KAL-EL LEAVING *KRYPTON* FOR A CHANCE AT A BETTER LIFE ON *EARTH*.

"EL" IS A HEBREW NAME-SUFFIX MEANING "ASCENSION" OR "GOD."

SIEGEL AND SHUSTER WERE BOTH KIDS OF JEWISH IMMIGRANTS-- SENSITIVE ABOUT THE EXPECTATIONS PUT ON THEM TO MAKE IT IN AMERICA.

SO SUPERMAN, EVEN THOUGH HE'S FROM ANOTHER WORLD, IS LIKE THE BEST CITIZEN OF HIS SOCIETY.

ANYONE WITH THE WILL CAN *MAKE* IT HERE.

THAT'S *CRAP*.

THAT'S THE *MYTH* OF AMERICA. BUT SUPERMAN DOESN'T USE HUMAN VIRTUES, HE USES ALIEN TRUMP CARDS.

HE BEATS THE CRAP OUT OF PEOPLE WHO DON'T PLAY THE GAME HIS WAY.

THIS IS SO COOL!

HE FIGHTS FOR THE AMERICAN *IDEAL*, BUT HE FIGHTS WITH HIS *FISTS*.

HE'S AN ALIEN INTERLOPER. *AND* HE'S AFTER OUR *WOMEN*.

HE'S A *FARMER'S* SON. HE'S AFTER *ONE* WOMAN. SAME AS ANY GUY WOULD BE.

BUT HE'S NOT ANY "GUY." HE'S "SUPER-MAN." HE'S *SUPERIOR*.

HE'S NOT SHOWING *US* WHAT *WE* CAN BE, BECAUSE WE CAN'T BE FROM ANOTHER PLANET, HAVE X-RAY VISION, FLIGHT, OR SUPER-*STRENGTH* AND--

HAVE YOU EVER *READ* THE COMIC?

WHAT'S *THAT* SUPPOSED TO MEAN?

YOU'RE TALKING ABOUT SUPERMAN LIKE HE'S THE *ENEMY*--OVER-THINKING HIM--

HEY, RELAX--

DON'T *TELL* ME HOW I'M *THINK-ING*!

--I'M JUST SUGGESTING THAT YOU MAY NOT KNOW--

49

SECRET IDENTITY

POWER

PERFECT

62

HIDDEN

IN A DREAM, I WAKE... READY TO CONFRONT THE DAY AND ITS CHALLENGES.

I AM, FOR ONCE, SUPREMELY CONFIDENT.

BUT AS THE DOOR CLOSES BEHIND ME, I REALIZE I'VE LEFT MY KEYS INSIDE.

I'M LOCKED OUT. AND WORSE...

...I'VE SOMEHOW FORGOTTEN TO DRESS.

I AM COMPLETELY NAKED.

FOR SOME REASON I SEE NO WAY TO REGAIN ENTRY AND FEEL I HAVE NO CHOICE BUT TO TRY TO MAKE IT THROUGH THE DAY...EXPOSED...

...HOPING NO ONE WILL NOTICE...

...HOPING TO HIDE IN PLAIN SIGHT...

...HOPING IN VAIN.

There was a hole
in the heart of
the world

A rip in the
promise of
tomorrow

Someone had taken all
the Earth's lives in
their hands

And clenched
their fists

One man

One mad man

One madman

There was a hole in
the heart of a hero

A sick certainty this harm
could not be put right

Somehow all
that was would
end, and nothing
could alter that

He clenched
his fists

This man

This super man

This Superman

At the end of the day   At the end of the world   What is justice?

The superman could hurl the madman into the abyss he had opened

Is justice the fierce pain of flesh scalded from bone by sulfuric steam?

Is justice the coarse collision of meat and bone with magma and base rock?

The superman could force the madman to witness the final days of the planet he had crippled

Is justice the realization that one has brought doom to that which gave him life?

Is justice living out the life sentence he has condemned others to serve?

Or is justice nothing more than an ideal?

Which, after a point, becomes purely

Academic

NIETZSCHE

This is the town of Röcken, Prussia.

It is in this place that Friedrich Nietzsche will be born to a Lutheran minister and his wife in the year of 1844.

He will not live to see the new millennium commence on January 1st, 1901.

But between his unceremonious birth and preemptive death, Nietzsche will provoke humanity with ideas as old as Plato's Republic, yet new as a moment.

Among his revelatory considerations? "Man," Nietzsche will say, though in very different words, "has within him the ability to set aside the traditional values...

"...Gentility...

"...Kindness...

"...Compassion...

"...and replace these 'antiquated' notions with alternative values that better serve man's desires...

"...Work...

"...Action...

"...Chaos."

"So long as guided by rational thought, man can thus define his world, not by tradition, but by those values that truly matter to him.

"Values he arrives at through internal discourse.

"Values which may be the values of no other man, but which are right and correct for him who claims them. This he may call 'the will to power.'

"In mastering this task," Nietzsche will say, though in a language different from this, "Man can become Übermensch."

Though the term means "over-man," Western translators will interpret it as "superman," a word which will stick.

Though some of its radical revisionism concerning man's ultimate values will be lost in the translation.

COURAGE

What is it with you, Nelson Corby?

Twilight was supposed to find you dining at "Nemo's" with your assistant, Nora.

Nora, who you hoped to finally muster the nerve to ask on a date after months of practicing the proposition in your midtown Metropolis mirror.

But an overtime meeting means a burger alone, a cab ride home, and another long, lonely shower.

It also means the chance for you to make a difference in someone's life.

And all it requires... is courage.

If the girl is to live, someone has to challenge the rushing bus.

Someone must be willing to risk his own life to earn a chance at saving hers.

Who will that someone be?

Not you, Nelson. You've long suspected, but learned today-- conclusively--

--that most hearts hold so much courage... but only so much, and then no more.

88

FORTRESS OF SOLITUDE

What the old man most desired was solitude.

He yearned to commit himself wholly to consideration of the great philosophical questions of his modern times.

But the world of his construction--wife Lotte, children Ernst and Gretl-- were of great distraction to his ruminations.

And so the old man moved far away, without telling family or friends that he was leaving.

He took a menial job and earned money enough to subsist on while completing his metaphysical considerations.

But as his fellow workers came to know him, they began to speak pleasantries and invite him to social gatherings.

Angered, the old man relocated to a cramped, windowless storage room in the rear of the facility.

Far from the others, he was content once more...until a janitor found his hidden workplace and began to service it.

Troubled by this minor intrusion, the old man quit his job altogether.

93

Relieved of his burden of work, he pondered at home in sublime silence.

But gradually, he became aware of the noise of his upstairs neighbors.

The old man built an extra ceiling—thick enough to eradicate all sounds of life above him.

The old man boarded over his windows.

Even so, there still persisted shadows of shuffling feet just beneath his door.

Unfortunately, flailing trees in noisy winds beyond his walls soon proved equal interruptions.

He sealed it off, first with bundled cloth and eventually mortar.

The old man sat in blissful stillness...until the hum of electric lights overhead became as deafening as any intruding voice.

He shattered the bulbs with a hammer.

94

Lying in his bed, there arose the chirps of crickets in the walls.

The old man fumigated with a poison he found in his pantry.

The sealed apartment retained the fumes at full potency for many, many days and the insects eventually died.

Finally...silence, but the old man could no longer hear, see, read, or even think clearly.

But a great notion did occur to him in this moment.

A man without human contact is a man without aid, without hope, without life.

The old man called for those around him, but the fortress of his own making swallowed all sound.

He could no longer be heard, but he had finally found what he had so long sought...

...perfect lasting solitude.

ALTERNATE REALITY

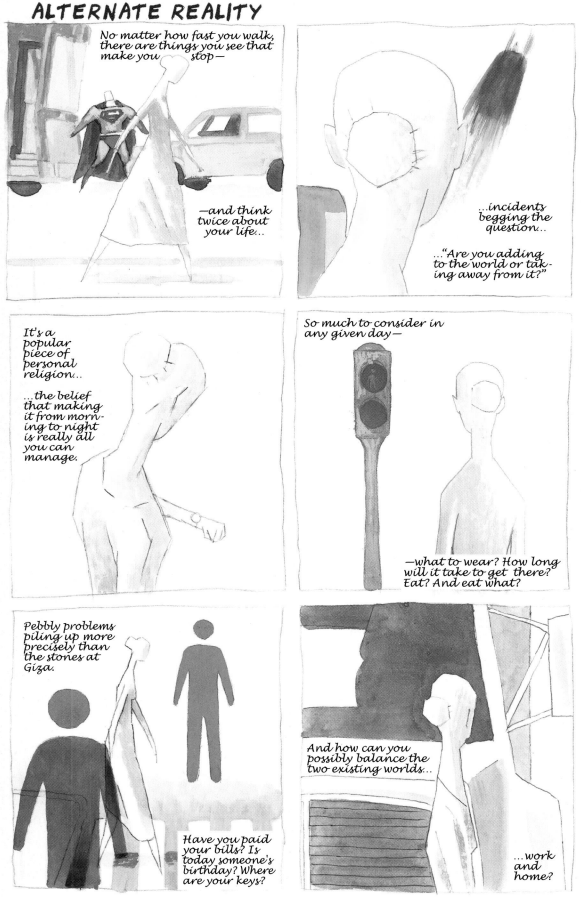

No matter how fast you walk, there are things you see that make you stop—

—and think twice about your life...

...incidents begging the question...

..."Are you adding to the world or taking away from it?"

It's a popular piece of personal religion...

...the belief that making it from morning to night is really all you can manage.

So much to consider in any given day—

—what to wear? How long will it take to get there? Eat? And eat what?

Pebbly problems piling up more precisely than the stones at Giza.

Have you paid your bills? Is today someone's birthday? Where are your keys?

And how can you possibly balance the two existing worlds...

...work and home?

But there are more worlds than just the little one that's fractaling around you faster than you care to notice...

..."alternative universes" where people pick through trash cans to decide what to wear or eat...

...townships where there are no bills because there is nothing to buy...

...villages where children don't consider their births the least bit worth celebrating...

...cities where keys are as moot as the doors they might unlock.

These things remind us that it is not people from another planet who are supermen...

...it is any individual able to see past their own little world...and reach out to the alternate ones beyond their limited scope of existence.

YEAH, WE'RE IN THE NEIGHBORHOOD NOW, MA...UH-HUH...

...WE'LL CALL IF WE FIND HIM...LOVE YOU *TOO*. BYE.

I HAD MA CHECK THE *CREDIT CARD* BILLS.

DAD CHARGED SOME DRINKS AT THIS PLACE HERE. LET'S GO IN AND ASK AROUND.

YOU'RE PRETTY *CLEVER* FOR AN ELECTRICIAN...

SO WHY *DO* I THINK I KNOW BETTER?

PROBABLY BECAUSE MY DAYS REVOLVE AROUND MAKING *DECISIONS* ABOUT PEOPLE--

SEEN THIS GUY AROUND HERE...?

--*IMAGINARY* PEOPLE, BUT ONES WHO CAN'T JUST UP AND VANISH UNLESS I *MAKE* THEM.

I HAVE TO DECIDE *EVERYTHING* FOR THEM--WHERE THEY *LIVE*, WHAT THEY *DO*, WHAT THEY *SAY*.

...LOOKING FOR OUR DAD...

WRITING CHARACTERS IS LIKE RAISING KIDS, ONLY MORE WORK--

--BECAUSE YOU HAVE TO DO *EVERYTHING* FOR THEM.

I GUESS IT'S POSSIBLE THAT MY WORK MIGHT *OCCASIONALLY* SEEP OUT INTO MY DAILY LIFE.

...SEEN HIM HERE LATELY?

SURE! EDDIE! HE'S, UH...

...HE WAS GOIN' TO, UH, SEE HIS *SIS*.

KNOW *WHERE?*

PLACE AROUN' THE CORNER. SUMMERFEST. SOME REHAB OR SOME SUCH.

I'LL POINT THE WAY IF YOU'LL BUY ME A DRINK!

103

"S"

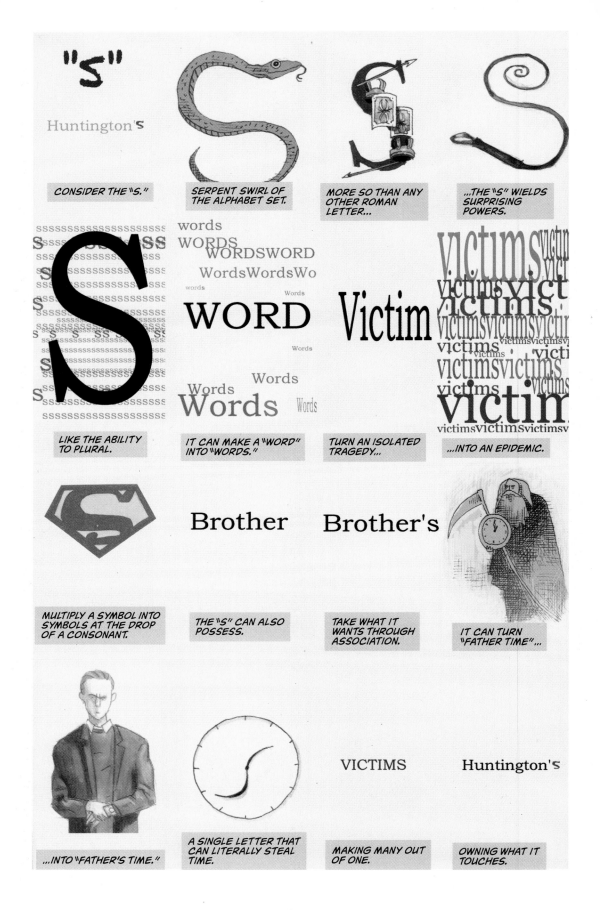

Huntington'**s**

CONSIDER THE "S."

SERPENT SWIRL OF THE ALPHABET SET.

MORE SO THAN ANY OTHER ROMAN LETTER...

...THE "S" WIELDS SURPRISING POWERS.

WORD

Victim

LIKE THE ABILITY TO PLURAL.

IT CAN MAKE A "WORD" INTO "WORDS."

TURN AN ISOLATED TRAGEDY...

...INTO AN EPIDEMIC.

Brother

Brother's

MULTIPLY A SYMBOL INTO SYMBOLS AT THE DROP OF A CONSONANT.

THE "S" CAN ALSO POSSESS.

TAKE WHAT IT WANTS THROUGH ASSOCIATION.

IT CAN TURN "FATHER TIME"...

VICTIMS

Huntington'**s**

...INTO "FATHER'S TIME."

A SINGLE LETTER THAT CAN LITERALLY STEAL TIME.

MAKING MANY OUT OF ONE.

OWNING WHAT IT TOUCHES.

NN*HHH*NN*NN!*

SHHHH... IT'S OKAY...IT'S ALL RIGHT...

WHAT YOU SEE, IMMEDIATELY...WHAT YOU KNOW...IS THAT THERE'S NO GOOD THING TO HOPE FOR A HUNTINGTON'S PATIENT.

IF YOU HOPE THEY'RE FINE EXCEPT FOR THEIR *BODY*--YOU'RE CONDEMNING THEM TO A LIFE SENTENCE LIVED OUT INSIDE A USELESS SHELL.

YOU CAN SHIELD A *CHILD'S* EYES FROM THIS...

...BUT AS AN *ADULT*, THERE IS NO *LOOK-ING AWAY.*

AND THE CONCERNS *COMPOUND* WHEN YOU OWN UP TO THE FACT THAT IN ANOTHER TWENTY YEARS...

...THIS COULD POSSIBLY BE *YOU...*

IF YOU HOPE THEY'RE VEGETATIVE AND MENTALLY *GONE*--

--THEN YOU'VE DAMNED THEM TO A MEANINGLESS LIVING DEATH.

...WITH YOUR KIDS LOOKING DOWN AT *YOUR* TWISTING, WRITHING BODY AND WONDERING THE SAME THINGS ABOUT YOU...

...AND *THEM-SELVES*...

...BECAUSE THIS IS NOT A CONDITION YOU COULD HIDE LIKE A RASH, OR A TUMOR SECRETED ON THE INSIDE.

THIS DISEASE SETS YOU *APART* MARKS YOU AS *DIFFERENT*...

...*ALIEN*...

THE ALIEN

HEY, SUPERMAN! YEAH, YOU! WHO YOU TRYIN' TO KID, KID? WHAT YOU TRYIN' TO PULL? WHAT YOU TAKE ME FOR, A FULL-ON SORE? MY EYES AIN'T X-RAY, BUT THEY SEE RIGHT THROUGH YOU.

YES, I'M TALKING TO YOUR KRYPTONIAN POMPADOUR, SLICK, WALKING THE STREETS LIKE YOU'RE KING SPIT, LOOKIN' FOR SOMEONE MORE OUTRAGEOUS TO HIT AND MAYBE HIDE BEHIND A BIT.

IN CASE YOU DIDN'T CHECK YOUR PASS-PORT STAMP, GOT MIXED UP WALKING DOWN THE DEEP SPACE EXIT RAMP, LET ME TELL YOU TRUE--

--YOU'RE AN ALIEN, FOOL!

YOU KNOW HOW MANY OTHER ALIENS ARE HOPIN' TO MAKE IT HERE, BUT HIDE IN FEAR BECAUSE WHAT MAKES THEM DIFFERENT MAKES THEM TARGETS TOO?

STAND-INS FOR STANDOUTS, FORCED TO ASK FOR HANDOUTS 'CAUSE THE LAND OF THE FREE AIN'T AS OFTEN BRAVE AND PUTS DEMANDS OUT TO HAVE THEM REMOVED.

HUNTED BY THE I.N.S., HOUNDED BY RACIST DURESS, THE UNFEELING, UNCARING, INSENSITIVE MESS OF MANKIND WITH NOTHING BETTER TO DO, BUT THEY MISSED YOU?

KRYPTONIAN, PLEASE!

YOU'VE GOT LIKE, WHAT? FOUR HEARTS, X-RAY EYES, SUPER DUPER HEAT VISION DELUXE, AND GREEN BLOOD TO BOOT.

WEARIN' YOUR PAJAMAS COLORED LIKE THE BAHAMAS, SAVIN' BOYS AN' GIRLS, DADDIES AND MOMMAS, STOPPIN' SUPER VILLAINS WITH THEIR EYES ON METRO'S LOOT?

AND THE ONLY HEAD YOU TURN IS LOIS LANE'S? THAT'S PROFANE, YOU'RE A METAPHOR FOR "NO WAY JACK," A FACT ATTACK, WHICH IS LIKE A HEART BUT HITS THE CORE OF ALL THAT'S TRUE--

--LIKE I'D LIKE TO HIT YOU.

IF YOU WERE JUST A LITTLE REALER, A LIVING BREATHING FEELER WITH CORPOREAL FORM THAT COULD CONNECT WITH MY LEFT HOOK, YOU COMIC BOOK CROOK--

--STOLE MY FAITH IN ALIEN INVASION AS YOU COMPLACENTLY VACATION AND OCCASIONALLY POP LUTHOR IN THE JAW OR LET MXYZPTLK HEM AND HAW AND ALL SO YOU CAN STAY--

--TAKE A PAGE FROM ME AND GET IN TOUCH WITH REALITY WHERE FOLKS WITH DIFFERENCES ARE TREATED EGREGIOUSLY, SET APART FROM YOU AND ME, NO MAKE THAT JUST ME--

--'CAUSE YOU DON'T REALLY BELONG HERE, SEE?

ESCAPE

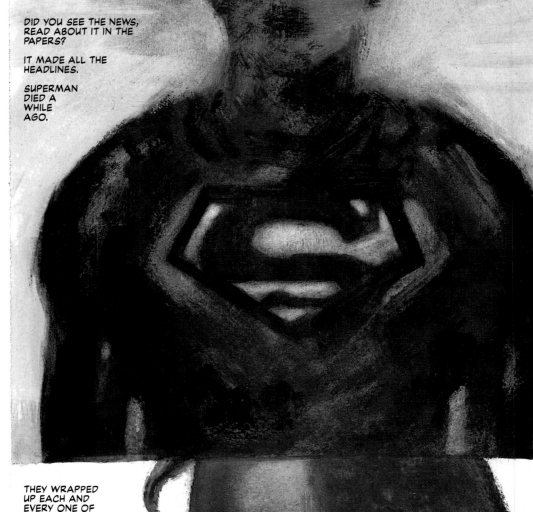

DID YOU SEE THE NEWS, READ ABOUT IT IN THE PAPERS?

IT MADE ALL THE HEADLINES.

SUPERMAN DIED A WHILE AGO.

THEY WRAPPED UP EACH AND EVERY ONE OF HIS ADVENTURES IN A BLACK PLASTIC COFFIN...

...AND BURIED HIM, HIS COSTUME, HIS HISTORY, AND HIS LEGEND...

...IN ABOUT 6 MILLION HOUSEHOLD PLOTS.

BUT IN HIS DARKEST HOUR,
WHEN IT SEEMED HE'D
FINALLY MET HIS MATCH,
SUPERMAN RETURNED.

SOME FELT THERE WAS
NO TRUTH OR JUSTICE
TO A STORY WHERE A
MAN COULD COME
BACK FROM THE
DEAD.

THERE'D ONLY BEEN ONE
OTHER BESTSELLER IN
HISTORY TO USE THAT
PLOT SUCCESSFULLY.

BUT THE WILLFUL USE OF THE
IMPOSSIBLE IS EXACTLY WHAT
COMIC BOOK STORIES ARE FOR...

...TO REMIND US THAT WHEN THE
REAL WORLD IS TOO MUCH TO
TAKE, THERE'S ALWAYS A PLACE
WE CAN GO...

...WHERE MAN, OR
SUPERMAN, CAN
ESCAPE ANYTHING
SET AGAINST HIM.

IN MY FATHER I SUDDENLY REALIZE WHAT IT IS **I'VE** BEEN FIGHTING.

I RECOGNIZE HIS RAGE BECAUSE...IT LOOKS JUST LIKE MY **OWN**.

I SEE IT FOR WHAT IT IS NOW...

...SHAME.

HE WANTS TO **ESCAPE** IT.

HE WANTS TO LIVE IN A FANTASY WORLD WHERE IF NO ONE SEES THE DISEASE IN HIS FAMILY, IT WON'T **EXIST**.

HE WANTS TO PRETEND THE DISEASE **SKIPPED** HIS GENERATION.

BUT HIS **SISTER** IS PROOF THAT IT DIDN'T.

MOST OF ALL, HE DOESN'T WANT TO HAVE TO ADMIT TO HIMSELF THAT HE MIGHT HAVE DOOMED HIS OWN CHILDREN...

...SIMPLY BY **HAVING** THEM.

THE FIRST SUPERMAN STORY I EVER READ WAS AT THE HOSPITAL THE DAY MY GRANDMOTHER DIED.

AFTER I HEARD WHAT MY DAD SAID TO AUNT SARAH, I STARTED READING THE COMIC INTENSELY SO HE WOULDN'T KNOW I'D HEARD HIM.

HERE'S WHAT I REMEMBER OF THAT STORY...

HERO

THIS VILLAIN CALLED **THE HUNTER**--WHO ACTS EVIL BY UNLEASHING WILD ANIMALS IN PUBLIC PLACES--

--TURNS HIS BEST FINDS EVER--THREE TERRIBLE CREATURES, A **GRIFFIN,** SOME KIND OF ANGRY **UNICORN,** AND SOMETHING CALLED A **BASILISK**--LOOSE ON METROPOLIS WITH NO PRIOR WARNING.

NOR DID I RATIONALIZE THAT SUPERMAN COULD HAVE SNUFFED THE HUNTER OUT LIKE A GNAT AFTER THEIR FIRST MEETING.

I LET THE STORY TAKE ME INTO IT...

AS THE PAGES ROLLED BY, I BOUGHT INTO THE CRISIS... BELIEVED IN THE DANGER...

AND AT THE END, THOUGH I NEVER WOULD HAVE ADMITTED IT...I WAS EMOTIONALLY INVESTED.

I WANTED TO TURN THE PAGE AND KNOW WHAT WAS GOING TO HAPPEN NEXT.

WHICH IS THE LESSON STORIES CAN TEACH LIFE.

THERE'S ALWAYS A "NEXT." ALWAYS.

THAT'S WHAT SUPERMAN IS ALL ABOUT. TO REMIND US THAT WE HAVE HURDLES...

...BUT AS LONG AS WE KEEP JUMPING THEM...

...WE'RE IN THE RACE.

Look! Up in the sky!

writer **Steven T. Seagle**
artist **Teddy Kristiansen**

letterer:
Todd Klein
superman created by
Jerry Siegel
and Joe Shuster

Day of admittance
May 5.

Diagnosis

HUNTINGTON'S

REMARKS/ TEST RESU

NAME

This book is for my Aunt Sarah who,
unfortunately, did not get to see it.
— *Steve Seagle*

To Hope, with love and thanks.
— *Teddy Kristiansen*

Teddy H. Kristiansen lives in Copenhagen, Denmark with the love of his life, Hope; his lovely daughters, Emily, Sophia, and Lulu; and his cats, Tigger and Mini. His Vertigo comics work includes HOUSE OF SECRETS: FOUNDATION and HOUSE OF SECRETS: FAÇADE (both with writer Steven T. Seagle); SANDMAN; and SANDMAN MIDNIGHT THEATRE. He has also illustrated Grendel: Four Devils, One Hell; Tarzan, and SUPERMAN: METROPOLIS. His first published work being an original Superman graphic album available only in Europe, IT'S A BIRD... marks a trip full circle of sorts for the artist. A man of many hats, Kristiansen has also worked in animation as well as commercial illustration, children's book illustration and the fine arts. His newest medium is plaster. More of his work can be found on his website, www.teddyk.dk. Next on his horizon is an issue of SOLO for DC Comics, a work which he is very proud of. He acknowledges some of the years it took him to paint this story in twenty-one distinctly different styles, but only some.

Steven T. Seagle lives in Pasadena, California with the love of his life, Liesel, and the cat of his life, Gaudi. His Vertigo comics work includes HOUSE OF SECRETS: FOUNDATION and HOUSE OF SECRETS: FAÇADE (both with artist Teddy Kristiansen); the multi-Eisner nominated SANDMAN MYSTERY THEATRE; and VERTICAL. He has also written such mainstays as Uncanny X-Men and SUPERMAN. His other writing venues include feature film, television, and, with his partners at Man of Action Studios LLC, animation and video games. His newest venture, SpeakTheaterArts.com, is writing and producing live theater in Los Angeles. He acknowledges some similarities between himself and the character "Steve" in this book, but only some.

Look for these other VERTIGO books:

All Vertigo titles are Suggested for Mature Readers

100 BULLETS
Brian Azzarello/Eduardo Risso
With one special briefcase, Agent Graves gives you the chance to kill without retribution. But what is the real price for this chance — and who is setting it?
Vol 1: FIRST SHOT, LAST CALL
Vol 2: SPLIT SECOND CHANCE
Vol 3: HANG UP ON THE HANG LOW
Vol 4: A FOREGONE TOMORROW
Vol 5: THE COUNTERFIFTH DETECTIVE
Vol 6: SIX FEET UNDER THE GUN

ANIMAL MAN
Grant Morrison/Chas Truog/
Doug Hazlewood/various
A minor super-hero's consciousness is raised higher and higher until he becomes aware of his own fictitious nature in this revolutionary and existential series.
Vol 1: ANIMAL MAN
Vol 2: ORIGIN OF THE SPECIES
Vol 3: DEUS EX MACHINA

THE BOOKS OF MAGIC
Neil Gaiman/various
A quartet of fallen mystics introduce the world of magic to young Tim Hunter, who is destined to become the world's most powerful magician.

THE BOOKS OF MAGIC
John Ney Rieber/Peter Gross/various
The continuing trials and adventures of Tim Hunter, whose magical talents bring extra trouble and confusion to his adolescence.
Vol 1: BINDINGS
Vol 2: SUMMONINGS
Vol 3: RECKONINGS
Vol 4: TRANSFORMATIONS
Vol 5: GIRL IN THE BOX
Vol 6: THE BURNING GIRL
Vol 7: DEATH AFTER DEATH

DEATH: AT DEATH'S DOOR
Jill Thompson
Part fanciful manga retelling of the acclaimed THE SANDMAN: SEASON OF MISTS and part original story of the party from Hell.

DEATH: THE HIGH COST OF LIVING
Neil Gaiman/Chris Bachalo/
Mark Buckingham
One day every century, Death assumes mortal form to learn more about the lives she must take.

DEATH: THE TIME OF YOUR LIFE
Neil Gaiman/Chris Bachalo/
Mark Buckingham/Mark Pennington
A young lesbian mother strikes a deal with Death for the life of her son in a story about fame, relationships, and rock and roll.

FABLES
Bill Willingham/Lan Medina/
Mark Buckingham/Steve Leialoha
The immortal characters of popular fairy tales have been driven from their homelands, and now live hidden among us, trying to cope with life in 21st-century Manhattan.
Vol 1: LEGENDS IN EXILE
Vol 2: ANIMAL FARM

HELLBLAZER
Jamie Delano/Garth Ennis/Warren Ellis/ Brian Azzarello/Steve Dillon/
Marcelo Frusin/various
Where horror, dark magic, and bad luck meet, John Constantine is never far away.
Vol 1: ORIGINAL SINS
Vol 2: DANGEROUS HABITS
Vol 3: FEAR AND LOATHING
Vol 4: TAINTED LOVE
Vol 5: DAMNATION'S FLAME
Vol 6: RAKE AT THE GATES OF HELL
Vol 7: HAUNTED
Vol 8: HARD TIME
Vol 9: GOOD INTENTIONS
Vol 10: FREEZES OVER

THE INVISIBLES
Grant Morrison/various
The saga of a terrifying conspiracy and the resistance movement combating it — a secret underground of ultra-cool guerrilla cells trained in ontological and physical anarchy.
Vol 1: SAY YOU WANT A REVOLUTION
Vol 2: APOCALIPSTICK
Vol 3: ENTROPY IN THE U.K.
Vol 4: BLOODY HELL IN AMERICA
Vol 5: COUNTING TO NONE
Vol 6: KISSING MR. QUIMPER
Vol 7: THE INVISIBLE KINGDOM

LUCIFER
Mike Carey/Peter Gross/
Scott Hampton/Chris Weston/
Dean Ormston/various
Walking out of Hell (and out of the pages of THE SANDMAN), an ambitious Lucifer Morningstar creates a new cosmos modeled after his own image.
Vol 1: DEVIL IN THE GATEWAY
Vol 2: CHILDREN AND MONSTERS
Vol 3: A DALLIANCE WITH THE DAMNED
Vol 4: THE DIVINE COMEDY
Vol 5: INFERNO

PREACHER
Garth Ennis/Steve Dillon/various
A modern American epic of life, death, God, love, and redemption — filled with sex, booze, and blood.
Vol 1: GONE TO TEXAS
Vol 2: UNTIL THE END OF THE WORLD
Vol 3: PROUD AMERICANS
Vol 4: ANCIENT HISTORY
Vol 5: DIXIE FRIED
Vol 6: WAR IN THE SUN
Vol 7: SALVATION
Vol 8: ALL HELL'S A-COMING
Vol 9: ALAMO

THE SANDMAN
Neil Gaiman/various
One of the most acclaimed and celebrated comics titles ever published.
Vol 1: PRELUDES & NOCTURNES
Vol 2: THE DOLL'S HOUSE
Vol 3: DREAM COUNTRY
Vol 4: SEASON OF MISTS
Vol 5: A GAME OF YOU
Vol 6: FABLES & REFLECTIONS
Vol 7: BRIEF LIVES
Vol 8: WORLDS' END

Vol 9: THE KINDLY ONES
Vol 10: THE WAKE
Vol 11: ENDLESS NIGHTS

SWAMP THING: DARK GENESIS
Len Wein/Berni Wrightson
A gothic nightmare is brought to life with this horrifying yet poignant story of a man transformed into a monster.

SWAMP THING
Alan Moore/Stephen Bissette/
John Totleben/Rick Veitch/various
The writer and the series that revolutionized comics — a masterpiece of lyrical fantasy.
Vol 1: SAGA OF THE SWAMP THING
Vol 2: LOVE & DEATH
Vol 3: THE CURSE
Vol 4: A MURDER OF CROWS
Vol 5: EARTH TO EARTH
Vol 6: REUNION

TRANSMETROPOLITAN
Warren Ellis/Darick Robertson/various
An exuberant trip into a frenetic future, where outlaw journalist Spider Jerusalem battles hypocrisy, corruption, and sobriety.
Vol 1: BACK ON THE STREET
Vol 2: LUST FOR LIFE
Vol 3: YEAR OF THE BASTARD
Vol 4: THE NEW SCUM
Vol 5: LONELY CITY
Vol 6: GOUGE AWAY
Vol 7: SPIDER'S THRASH
Vol 8: DIRGE
Vol 9: THE CURE

Y: THE LAST MAN
Brian K. Vaughan/Pia Guerra/
José Marzán, Jr.
An unexplained plague kills every male mammal on Earth — all except Yorick Brown and his pet monkey. Will he survive this new, emasculated world to discover what killed his fellow men?
Vol 1: UNMANNED
Vol 2: CYCLES

BARNUM!
Howard Chaykin/David Tischman/Niko Henrichon

BLACK ORCHID
Neil Gaiman/Dave McKean

HEAVY LIQUID
Paul Pope

HOUSE OF SECRETS: FOUNDATIONS

HOUSE OF SECRETS: FACADE
Steven T. Seagle/Teddy Kristiansen

HUMAN TARGET
Peter Milligan/Edvin Biukovic

HUMAN TARGET: FINAL CUT
Peter Milligan/Javier Pulido

I DIE AT MIDNIGHT
Kyle Baker

IN THE SHADOW OF EDGAR ALLAN POE
Jonathon Scott Fuqua/
Stephen John Phillips/Steven Parke

JONNY DOUBLE
Brian Azzarello/Eduardo Risso

KING DAVID
Kyle Baker

MR. PUNCH
Neil Gaiman/Dave McKean

THE MYSTERY PLAY
Grant Morrison/Jon J Muth

THE NAMES OF MAGIC
Dylan Horrocks/Richard Case

NEIL GAIMAN & CHARLES VESS' STARDUST
Neil Gaiman/Charles Vess

NEIL GAIMAN'S MIDNIGHT DAYS
Neil Gaiman/Matt Wagner/various

ORBITER
Warren Ellis/Colleen Doran

PREACHER: DEAD OR ALIVE (THE COLLECTED COVERS)
Glenn Fabry

PROPOSITION PLAYER
Bill Willingham/Paul Guinan/Ron Randall

THE SANDMAN: THE DREAM HUNTERS
Neil Gaiman/Yoshitaka Amano

THE SANDMAN: DUST COVERS — THE COLLECTED SANDMAN COVERS 1989-1997
Dave McKean/Neil Gaiman

THE SANDMAN PRESENTS: THE FURIES
Mike Carey/John Bolton

THE SANDMAN PRESENTS: TALLER TALES
Bill Willingham/various

SHADE, THE CHANGING MAN: THE AMERICAN SCREAM
Peter Milligan/Chris Bachalo

TRUE FAITH
Garth Ennis/Warren Pleece

UNCLE SAM
Steve Darnall/Alex Ross

UNDERCOVER GENIE
Kyle Baker

UNKNOWN SOLDIER
Garth Ennis/Kilian Plunkett

V FOR VENDETTA
Alan Moore/David Lloyd

VEILS
Pat McGreal/Stephen John Phillips/José Villarrubia

WHY I HATE SATURN
Kyle Baker

THE WITCHING HOUR
Jeph Loeb/Chris Bachalo/Art Thibert

YOU ARE HERE
Kyle Baker

Visit us at www.vertigocomics.com for more information on these and many other titles from VERTIGO and DC Comics or call 1-888-COMIC BOOK for the comics shop nearest you, or go to your local book store.

VER0014